Seeds of a Nation

Nevada

Bob Anderson

KIDHAVEN PRESS™

THOMSON
★ ™
GALE

San Diego • Detroit • New York • San Francisco • Cleveland
New Haven, Conn. • Waterville, Maine • London • Munich

© 2003 by KidHaven Press. KidHaven Press is an imprint of The Gale Group, Inc.,
a division of Thomson Learning, Inc.

KidHaven™ and Thomson Learning™ are trademarks used herein under license.

For more information, contact
KidHaven Press
27500 Drake Rd.
Farmington Hills, MI 48331-3535
Or you can visit our Internet site at http://www.gale.com

LIBRARY OF CONGRESS CATALOGING-IN-PUBLICATION DATA

Anderson, Bob, 1950–
  Nevada / by Bob Anderson.
    p. cm. — (Seeds of a nation)
  Summary: Discusses native peoples of Nevada and the history of the state's
  settlement.
  Includes bibliographical references and index.
  ISBN 0-7377-1564-2 (lib. bdg. : alk. paper)
  1. Nevada—History—Juvenile literature. 2. Nevada—Discovery and exploration—
  Juvenile literature. 3. Frontier and pioneer life—Nevada—Juvenile literature.
  I. Title. II. Series.
  F841.3.A84   2003
  979.3—dc21

  2002013086

Printed in China

Contents

Introduction

A Tide of Settlers

Nevada is a large state with a small population—
110,000 square miles and just under 2 million people. Many major cities in the United States have a larger population than the entire state of Nevada, yet Nevada could fit several eastern states within its borders. California borders Nevada to the west and south, Arizona and Utah lie east of it, and Oregon and Idaho sit on its northern border. The name Nevada comes from the Spanish word for "snow-covered." It was probably taken from the name of the large mountain range on the California-Nevada border. This mountain range is called by its Spanish name, **Sierra Nevada**.

Nevada is part of the Wild West. Its history reads much like a classic western movie. As in such movies, scenes in Nevada's history include cowboys and Indians, forts and cavalry, wagon trains and pioneers, **prospectors** and gold mines, **boomtowns** and ghost towns. And just like in the movies, Nevada's story is of good people versus bad people, greedy people and generous people, lucky people who make their fortunes, and unlucky people who lose everything.

U.S. history in Nevada—and much of the West—begins much later than the history of New England and the original thirteen colonies on the East Coast. The year the colonies declared themselves independent from Great Britain and fought the Revolutionary War—1776—was the same year the first European entered

Prospectors haul their equipment across a rocky landscape in search of gold in the West.

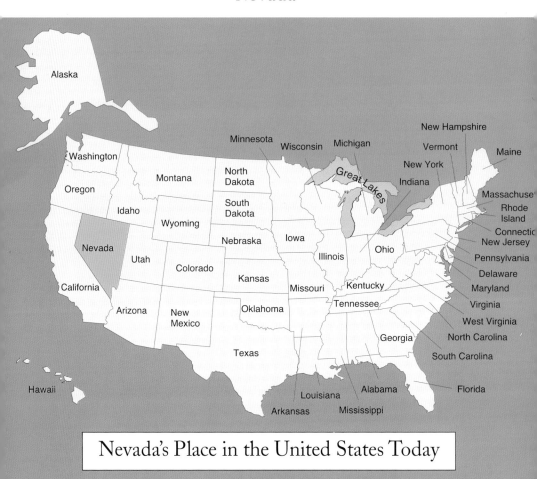

Nevada's Place in the United States Today

Nevada. And that European was a Spaniard from Mexico, not someone from the American colonies. White, or European, Americans did not find Nevada until a decade or two of the nineteenth century had passed, around 1820 or 1830. Up to that time, native peoples, often called Indians or Native Americans, were the only human **inhabitants** of Nevada.

The story of Nevada begins with the clash between native peoples whose cultures had existed almost unchanged for thousands of years and the arrival of

European settlers. The Europeans' goals were to conquer the land and use its riches of fur, timber, gold, and silver. The Europeans succeeded in their goal, and they then used those riches to create great cities, railroads, and commerce. The natives were outnumbered in just a few years and finally had to give in to the newcomers. Some of the natives fought back; others moved away. But neither of these responses held back the tide of settlers from the East. Nevada's story is a violent one. But perhaps the violence was just a part of the difficult beginning of the state of Nevada, one of the seeds of our nation.

Chapter One

Native Peoples of Nevada

Scientists believe that the first people to live in Nevada arrived about twelve thousand years ago, after the last Ice Age. Scientists know this because they have found stone tools and weapons left by these ancient peoples that date back to that time. Nevada's climate was very different then. Today, it is mostly unfriendly desert. But then, many lakes and wetlands left by the retreating glaciers dotted the land. That meant wild game and water were plentiful. Life for human inhabitants was not difficult.

The early natives often used the many caves found throughout Nevada for shelter. For food they gathered acorns, berries, pine nuts, and other wild plants. They also hunted ducks, deer, and rabbits, and fished for trout and salmon. Scientists have even found duck decoys used by these ancient hunters to lure ducks within range of their stone-tipped darts and spears.

But within a few hundred years, the climate began to change. It got drier. The lakes shrank or dried up. Rivers became little streams. Within two or three thousand years, Nevada looked like it does today—dry, rocky mountains and dusty valleys. The plants and animals the

The dry Valley of Fire spans southern Nevada. Native Americans settled in this harsh area around A.D. 1000.

natives used for food became less plentiful, and many people left the region for greener, cooler climates in the North and the East.

The harsh climate was difficult to survive in. Temperatures in the winter dropped below freezing and in the summer rose to as high as 120 degrees. Those who stayed had to change their lifestyles to survive. Instead of following migrating wild game or moving to where wild plants were ready to harvest, they stayed in one place. They learned to grow their own food, including corn, beans, and squash. Water, once plentiful, was very important for survival. As a result, most of the native peoples lived along the remaining rivers, lakes, or springs. In winter, they made cloaks of rabbit skins to keep warm. The rest of the time they wore very little, often just a small apron of woven grass.

For shelter, if no caves were nearby, the people built huts from willow branches and grass or reeds. Willow branches were used because they could be easily bent into shape without snapping. The branches were stuck into the ground in a circle, then tied together with thinner branches. The tops of the branches that were stuck in the ground were bent toward the center of the circle and tied together to form a dome-shaped structure. This was then covered with mats woven from tall grasses or river reeds.

The Lost City

About 300 B.C., or about twenty-three hundred years ago, a group of native people arrived from the East.

Native peoples built dome-shaped huts, similar to the one pictured here, when caves were not available for shelter.

They were called the Anasazi (pronounced an-uh-*sah*-zee). The Anasazi lived mostly in an area that today makes up the states of New Mexico, Arizona, and Colorado, but some of them moved west to Nevada. The Nevada Anasazi developed a rich culture of building, farming, mining, handicrafts, and trading.

In 1924 the remains of one of their villages was discovered along the Muddy River northeast of Las Vegas. Scientists called it Nevada's "Lost City" and explored the

Members of an Anasazi community go about their day among cliff housing.

remains hoping to find out more about this ancient people. Much of what was left of the village had been buried in the drifting desert sands. Their work was rewarded as they dug up ancient houses, storerooms, and a town square made of sun-dried mud bricks called **adobe** (pronounced uh-*doh*-bee). After years of digging at the site, scientists were able to put together a better picture of the ancient village. They found traces of corn in the adobe storerooms and pieces of cotton clothing in the houses. This meant that the Anasazi had learned to grow crops and store food for the winter and to weave cloth and sew it into clothing. The scientists determined that the community had lived there around the year A.D. 1000—about five hundred years before Christopher Columbus arrived in America. The waters of Lake Mead later covered the village after Hoover Dam was built in 1935.

Anasazi women grind corn that will later be used to make bread.

Before that happened, however, scientists re-created an exact copy of the village near the town of Overton. On this same site they also built a museum to display what they had found and to tell the Anasazi's story.

Scientists later found other similar communities. The collection of villages stretched for more than twenty-five miles along the Muddy and Virgin Rivers in southwestern Nevada. These riverside dwellers traded food, pottery, baskets, shells, salt, and obsidian, a glassy yet hard stone used for knives and arrowheads. They mined turquoise for jewelry and salt for preserving and seasoning food. They set up trading networks with their neighbors. They were also the first people to use **irrigation** for farming in the dry regions of the Southwest.

Sometime after the year A.D. 1100, the Anasazi simply disappeared, not only from Nevada but from everywhere. No one knows for sure why. Over the following centuries other native peoples moved into Nevada.

Five Groups

By 1776, when white Europeans first started to explore Nevada, five main groups of native peoples lived in Nevada: the Washo (pronounced *wah*-shoo), the Shoshone (pronounced sho-*sho*-nee), the Mojave (pronounced mo-*hav*-ee), the Northern Paiute (pronounced *pie*-oot), and the Southern Paiute. The Washo lived in the Sierra Nevada around Lake Tahoe at the western corner of the state, and the Shoshone lived across the center portion of the state. The Mojave lived in the stark desert of Death Valley and along the Colorado River in the southwestern area

The Mojave wore little clothing in the brutal heat of what is now Death Valley.

of Nevada. The Paiute settled both north and south of the Shoshone territory. All of these native tribes had moved into Nevada from farther east to avoid fighting with neighboring tribes that were moving into their territories. The different tribes would often raid each other's camps to steal food and tools and even people, whom they took to use as slaves.

The native peoples of Nevada were self-sufficient. They had learned not only how to find food, but also how to grow their own. They also used the raw materials provided by nature to make beautiful and useful items. When the European Americans arrived, the natives shared their knowledge with them and taught them how to survive, too. Unfortunately, the clash of these two very different cultures did not end well for the native peoples.

Chapter Two

Pioneers and Pathfinders

The first European explorers to enter what is now Nevada were Spanish. The Spanish had conquered and **colonized** Mexico centuries earlier, calling it New Spain. New Spain included the areas known today as Mexico, New Mexico, Arizona, California, and Texas.

In 1776, the thirteen American colonies on the East Coast were declaring their independence from Britain. That same year Spanish **missionaries** set off from Santa Fe, New Mexico, to find overland routes to their California settlements of Los Angeles and Monterey. During this trailblazing **expedition**, they crossed Nevada. These early trailblazers, like later ones, depended heavily on help from the native peoples they met. They first encountered the Southern Paiute, who had moved into Nevada to escape the Navajo and Ute invasions of their original territories to the East. The Paiute showed the missionaries the route through their territory. They also gave them food and supplies. This experience was repeated as the expedition entered Shoshone territory in central Nevada and Northern Paiute lands in the North. Because the missionaries received supplies and guidance from the native peoples, they were then able to survive passage across the forbidding deserts and mountains. They finally arrived at Monterey, California, thanks to their friendly guides. The route they mapped was later called the Old Spanish Trail. Their expedition is

A missionary enthusiastically preaches to a curious group in an effort to convert Native Americans to Christianity.

known today because they kept detailed diaries of their trip. Their records are the earliest sources of history for that area and are of great value to scientists today.

In the early 1800s the first European Americans from the United States began to explore the area that is now Nevada. They were looking for new sources of furs for their employers back East, the large fur-trading companies. Following the Humboldt River that passed through northern Nevada, the trappers and traders encountered the Northern Paiute and Shoshone. These two tribes had themselves migrated from the Great Plains to escape their more aggressive neighbors, the Crow and Blackfoot peoples. The native peoples still lived off the land by hunting and fishing and gathering wild plants and seeds, just as earlier natives had done. They traded beaver, muskrat, and rabbit furs to the white strangers in exchange for tools and weapons. The natives would often treat their guests to feasts of large trout they had caught in the nearby lakes and rivers. Native guides showed the explorers safely across the great mountain range of the Sierra Nevada into the rich forests of California.

John C. Frémont: "The Pathfinder"

One of the most famous explorers from the United States was John C. Frémont. Frémont's goal was different from that of the trailblazers before him. They had been searching for furs and routes to the West so they could claim territory for their fur-trading companies. Their dealings with the native peoples had been to trade for furs and to use them as guides. Frémont's goals, how-

A modern-day Blackfoot tribe member stands proudly in the traditional dress of his people.

ever, were different. He wanted to scout the **territories** in the West for future **conquest** by the United States. Until this time—the 1840s—these lands had been claimed by Mexico. But because the lands were not settled, Mexico did not really control them. Frémont wanted to claim them for the United States. To do this, he organized expeditions to map the territory and to find passages to the Pacific Coast. Frémont believed that a great river ran from the Rocky Mountains all the way to the Pacific

General John C. Frémont set out to explore Nevada in hopes of claiming land for the United States.

Ocean. If he could find this river, he would find easy passage to the coast. During his explorations, however, he noted that the rivers in the area did not flow toward the ocean but away from it. They ran east from the Sierra Nevada. He realized that the whole area was shaped like a giant bowl into which all the water sources drained. As a result, he named the area the Great Basin—a name still used today. Although he had discovered large, beautiful lakes in Nevada, including Lake Tahoe and Pyramid Lake, Frémont also discovered that no great river passage to the sea existed.

To aid him in successfully exploring Nevada and the Great Basin, Frémont hired mountain men Kit Carson and Joseph Walker, who knew how to read the land and how to survive on their own. To get the help of these top **frontiersmen**, Frémont paid them three times the going rate. In honor of their valuable help, he also renamed rivers, lakes, and even towns after them. Today Nevada has the Carson River, Walker Lake, and its capital, Carson City.

Chief Truckee

Another key figure in Frémont's success, as well as in the success of many other explorers passing through northern Nevada, was Truckee. He was the chief of the Northern Paiute, and he lived at the bottom of the eastern Sierra Nevada on the Humboldt Trail. Truckee is famous because he remained friendly with the white pioneers even when other natives grew **hostile** toward them. The white people did not understand the native people's ways and so often treated them badly, stole their belongings, and polluted their lands. Many native tribes became unfriendly toward pioneers, but Truckee insisted that his people continue to help them. Truckee even fought alongside John Frémont against the Mexicans during the Mexican-American War in the 1840s. Truckee's loyalty and leadership earned him the rank of captain in Frémont's army. He treasured his new name, Captain Truckee, for the rest of his life. Grateful pioneers also named a river and its valley and a town after the Paiute chief.

Kit Carson (pictured) helped Frémont explore Nevada. Carson City, the state's present-day capital, was named after him.

A painting illustrates a fierce battle between the two sides who fought in the Mexican-American War.

John Frémont's deeds were often reported in the big newspapers back East, and he soon became famous. People called him "The Pathfinder." He later became a U.S. senator from California and the first Republican candidate for president. Because of his reports, people living back East became more familiar with the unknown Wild West. They came to believe that they, too, could travel safely across the Great Basin and the Sierra Nevada. Hoping to find a new fortune in a new land, Easterners began moving to Nevada and California in ever-increasing numbers. In the last half of the 1800s, the Wild West would see a population explosion as settlers flocked to it.

Chapter Three

The First Settlers Arrive

The glorious reports of the trailblazers may have inspired many people to move west, but the reality of getting there was a different story. The passage to Nevada and California was not easy. Nor was it guaranteed to be successful. It took planning and patience, and not a little luck, to travel across the Great Plains and the Great Basin. And if that trip was successful, the Sierra Nevada still remained ahead. Crossing the snowcapped mountain range taxed people's courage and endurance to the utmost. Some did not pass the test.

The Donner Party

In 1846 a wagon train of eighty-seven people left Springfield, Illinois, for California. Most of the party was made up of two families, the Reeds and the Donners. George Donner, a sixty-two-year-old farmer, led the group. They made their way slowly across the Great Plains and into the

Great Basin. By the time they got to Nevada and had only the Sierra Nevada to cross, it was late October. The mountains were covered with snow clouds, and freezing temperatures greeted the travelers. Some wanted to wait, and others wanted to hurry ahead to beat the snowfall. They went

Members of the Donner party huddle for warmth in the bitter cold of the Sierra Nevada.

ahead. A thousand feet from the rocky summit, a blizzard hit them. The pass became blocked by snow. Their wagons and mules could not move. Their guide lost the path. They were trapped there for months before rescue teams could get to them. They had to eat their animals. Several of the party members died of hunger and exposure. Finally, desperate with hunger, the survivors had no choice but to eat the frozen bodies of their fallen companions. When all the survivors were finally rescued, it was late April. Of the eighty-seven persons who had left Illinois, only forty-six survived. Today, the mountain pass they could not reach is called Donner Pass.

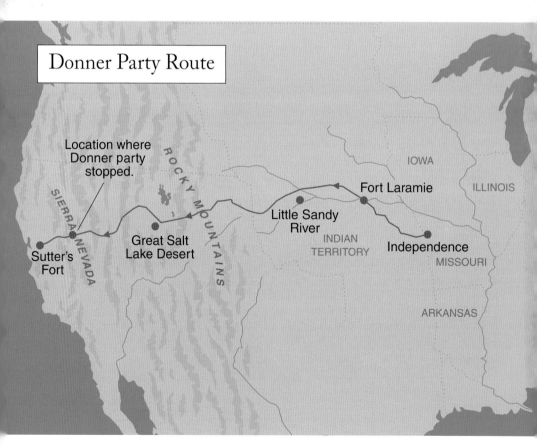

Donner Party Route

Location where Donner party stopped.

IOWA

Fort Laramie

ILLINOIS

SIERRA NEVADA

ROCKY MOUNTAINS

Little Sandy River

Sutter's Fort

Great Salt Lake Desert

INDIAN TERRITORY

Independence

MISSOURI

ARKANSAS

The story of the ill-fated Donner party has become legendary. It stands to this day as a witness and a warning to all who would attempt to face the awesome power of nature without sufficient knowledge and preparation. Nonetheless, the settlers came, driven by the lure of adventure, the fates of war, and even the voice of God.

On February 2, 1848, the United States and Mexico signed the Treaty of Guadalupe Hidalgo (pronounced Wad-ah-*loo*-pay Hee-*doll*-go) ending the Mexican-American

In the 1850s Brigham Young sent two groups to Nevada to set up way stations between California and Salt Lake City, Utah.

War. The terms of the treaty included Mexico's handing over to the United States land that is now the states of Texas, New Mexico, Arizona, California, and parts of Colorado, Utah, and Nevada. In 1850 the U.S. government established the Utah Territory, which covered most of today's states of Utah, Idaho, and Nevada. The request to become an official territory of the United States was made by Brigham Young, the leader of the Mormon Church in Salt Lake City, Utah. Mormons had been the first white settlers in Nevada. Their story is an important part of Nevada's history.

The Mormons

The Mormon Church was started in 1830 by a young man named Joseph Smith. He believed that God had told him to remake the Christian church according to the way Jesus Christ had intended it to be. According to Mormon teaching, an angel gave Smith a book titled *The Book of Mormon*, which, along with the Bible, Mormons accepted as the word of God. Hence, its members have come to be called Mormons. *The Book of Mormon* told of the lost tribes of Israel that had come to America during Old Testament times. The Mormons believed Native Americans were **descendants** of one of these lost tribes and must therefore accept Mormonism. This belief later played a key role in the Mormons' settlement of Utah and Nevada.

Joseph Smith tried many times to find a place where the members of his church could live according to their beliefs. In each place they settled, however, the local peoples disapproved of the Mormons' beliefs and drove them out of town. In 1844 the townspeople of Nauvoo, Illinois, killed Smith and his brother. To avoid further **persecution**, the new church leader, Brigham Young, led his followers out of the Midwest and far into the western wilderness away from non-Mormon settlements. In late 1847 they settled by the shores of the Great Salt Lake in what is now Utah. They were the first white settlement in the Great Basin.

In 1851 Brigham Young sent a group of his people, led by John Reese, west into the Carson River valley in what is now northern Nevada. Their mission was to build a way station for travelers to get supplies on the way from California to Salt Lake City and to convert the native people to Mormonism. The settlement was called Mormon Station and was the site of the first permanent building in Nevada.

A wagon train treks to the West to settle in Nevada and California.

Four years later Young sent another group of settlers to southern Nevada near present-day Las Vegas with the same mission: to build a way station and teach the natives about Mormonism. Young's plan was to set up a line of way stations from Los Angeles, California, to Salt Lake City. The way stations would help travelers on their hard journey across the wilderness. They would also serve as forts to defend the Mormons from further persecution by non-Mormons. The harsh environment of the Nevada desert, however, got the better of the settlers.

Mormons gather to discuss the issues of the day in front of a building used for church services.

A 150-year-old building in Genoa, Nevada, still stands today as a reminder of those who first settled the area.

Within two years they had abandoned the Las Vegas settlement and returned to Utah. The line of way stations never became a reality. What did become a reality, though, was a greater number of non-Mormons settling the Nevada territory.

More and more non-Mormons settled in Mormon Station in a short time because of its location. It was at the foot of the Sierra Nevada along the Humboldt Trail to California. It was a place for travelers to pick up more supplies and to rest before or after the difficult trip across the great mountain range. As it became less of a Mormon settlement, its name was changed to Genoa (pronounced Jeh-NO-uh), after the hometown of one of its Italian residents. In 1854 it became the county seat of Carson County in the Utah Territory and later, in 1861, the county seat of Douglas County in the Nevada Territory.

Genoa's fortunes soon changed, however. Because it was only a way station, a place for travelers to stop on their way farther west, Genoa grew very slowly. But before the end of the 1850s, thousands of people had settled in the territory. New towns sprang up quickly and gained more importance than Genoa. The reason for this was not gold, as in California, but silver.

Chapter Four

The Silver State

In 1849 the gold rush began. Thousands of prospectors called forty-niners passed through Nevada on their way to make their fortunes in the gold mines of California. Some gold was found in Nevada, too, as well as other valuable metals, such as silver, tin, lead, and copper. These minerals were important for many types of industry and manufacturing back East, as well as for daily life in Nevada.

Mining soon became an important industry all over Nevada. The short-lived Mormon mission sent by Brigham Young in 1855 to Las Vegas discovered a large lead deposit, which was mined for several years. Lead was necessary for making bullets, **pewter** for cups and plates, and other items. About the same time, gold was discovered in the Eldorado Canyon at the southern tip of Nevada. The Eldorado gold mines produced gold from 1860 to the 1940s.

Miners eagerly dig for silver in western Nevada. More silver was found there in 1859 than anywhere else in the world.

Many such mines were worked all over Nevada during and after the California gold rush. Towns sprang up around the mines because of the newfound wealth. Just as quickly, however, the mines gave out, the people left, and the shiny new towns became dusty, empty ghost towns. Many of these ghost towns still dot the Nevada landscape and are now popular tourist attractions.

By 1852 most of the gold in California had been mined and sent to banks back East and in Europe. The prospectors who were still hoping to strike it rich on their own left California and went anywhere gold was discovered, including Canada and even Australia. Then, in 1859, ten years after the California gold rush had drawn thousands of fortune hunters through Nevada, over the Sierra Nevada, into California, a new **lode** was found. This time it was in Nevada, only miles from the Carson Trail used by the forty-niners. It was not gold, but silver—tons and tons of it. It was the greatest silver find in history.

Miners dance and sing in celebration of their silver fortunes.

The Comstock Lode

Two Irish prospectors, Peter O'Reilly and Patrick McLaughlin, were panning for gold one spring day in 1859 on the eastern slopes of the Sierra Nevada near the area of present-day Reno. They found little gold but lots of heavy, blue-gray sand. Like so many earlier prospectors who had found the bluish substance in that area, they did not know what it was. O'Reilly and McLaughlin decided to have it tested. The test results showed it was silver sulfide (silver combined with sulfur) worth $4,000 a ton. Henry Comstock, a businessman, heard about the find and filed a claim for the land where the discovery had been made. He therefore legally owned the land and so the lode came to be named after him.

In the next year, seventeen thousand people came to the area to work the mines of the Comstock Lode. They lived in tents, wagons, wooden huts, and caves—anything they could find for shelter. Around them the town of Virginia City sprang up almost overnight, it seemed. Banks were built to process all the money. **Saloons**, gambling houses, and dance halls were opened to give the miners somewhere to amuse themselves and spend their money. Merchants arrived to provide goods for the miners and their families. And Nevada's first newspaper, the *Territorial Enterprise*, was started there. One of the newspaper's first reporters was a man named Samuel Clemens, who later wrote *The Adventures of Huckleberry Finn* and *The Adventures of Tom Sawyer* under the name Mark Twain.

Within just a couple of years, Virginia City's population swelled to nearly thirty thousand, making it the

Carriages roll through the busy town of Virginia City during the 1870s.

second-largest city in the West. The city had hotels, restaurants, and department stores that rivaled those in the great eastern cities of New York and Philadelphia. Its wealth overflowed into San Francisco on the other side of the Sierra Nevada as well, making that city a prosperous financial center and the largest city in the West.

Working the Mines

Despite the riches the silver brought to the region, the work of digging it out was hard and dangerous. The mines sometimes went as deep as three thousand feet, more than half a mile down. The temperature could reach 120 degrees. Great airshafts were sunk into the mines to provide fresh air to the miners, and tons of ice were used to cool them off. (Air-conditioning did not exist in the 1860s.) Many died from the harsh conditions, but most believed the risk was worth it because of the high pay they received. Before they were done, they would mine $400 million in silver and some gold from the lode. And unlike the gold from the California gold rush, which was sent back East and to Europe, most of the wealth from the Comstock Lode stayed in the West and helped build railroads and cities. It was the beginning of the development of the Wild West into civilized territory.

Battle Born

As Nevadans in the 1860s worked to develop their land in the far West, a political storm was building thousands of miles away in the East. The issues of slavery and states' rights were dividing the North from the South. In 1861 the conflict erupted into the Civil War. Most of the newly wealthy Nevadans were from the Northeast, and so they sided with the Union against the Confederacy. They sent great amounts of money to help the Union win the war. To ensure that Nevada's great wealth would remain part of the Union, President Abraham Lincoln wanted to grant it statehood right away. He personally rushed along the usually lengthy process. He also needed Nevada's vote in Congress to help pass the Thirteenth Amendment to the U.S. Constitution, which abolished slavery. A copy of Nevada's

Union troops say good-bye to their hometown before departing for battle during the Civil War.

Las Vegas, Nevada's largest city today, sparkles beneath a red and purple sunset.

state constitution was actually telegraphed to Washington, D.C., rather than mailed, which would have taken weeks to arrive. That set the record for the longest telegraph message ever sent! Nevada then became the thirty-sixth state of the Union on October 31, 1864.

Because Nevada became a state during the Civil War, its state slogan became Battle Born. And because the key to its fortune was its great mineral wealth—especially the Comstock Lode—Nevada's nickname became the Silver State. It became, and remains, a legendary place where fortunes can be won and lost in the twinkling of an eye.

Facts About Nevada

Capital city: **Carson City**

Largest city: **Las Vegas**

Area: **110,567 square miles (7th-largest state)**

Population: **1,998,257 (35th-largest state)**

State animal: **desert bighorn sheep**

State bird: **mountain bluebird**

State colors: **silver and blue**

State flower: **sagebrush**

State tree: **piñon pine**

Nicknames: **the Silver State; also the Sagebrush State**

State motto: **All for our country**

State slogan: **Battle Born**

Agricultural economy: **cattle, hay, dairy products, potatoes**

Industrial economy: **tourism, mining, machinery, printing and publishing, food processing, electric equipment**

Glossary

adobe: Desert building material made from sun-dried clay and straw.

boomtowns: Towns enjoying a rapid growth of business or population.

colonized: Settled by citizens of another country.

conquest: The act of defeating and taking control of another people.

descendants: People related through ancestry.

expedition: A planned journey taken for a special purpose.

frontiersmen: People who live in or explore the edges (frontier) of a territory.

hostile: Unfriendly.

inhabitants: People who live in a specific place.

irrigation: The process of bringing water from its source to another place without water.

lode: A large mineral deposit.

missionaries: People who try to convert other people into a religious belief.

pewter: A metal made from combining tin and lead.

prospectors: People who explore an area looking for mineral deposits.

persecution: To treat another unfairly because of his or her beliefs.

saloons: Drinking halls; bars.

Sierra Nevada: Mountain range along the California-Nevada border.

For Further Exploration

Books

Robert J. Franklin and Pamela A. Bunte, *The Paiute*. New York: Chelsea House, 1990. Includes a history of this Nevada people, their daily lives, a picture essay of baskets, and description of modern Paiute people.

Patricia Kummer, *Nevada*. Mankato, MN: Capstone High/Low Books, 1999. An overview of the history, geography, people, and living conditions of the state of Nevada.

Carole Marsh, *Nevada Hard to Believe (but True!) History, Mystery, Trivia, Legend, Lore & More*. Decatur, GA: Gallopade Publishing Group, 1990. A fun, easy-to-read book of incredible but true facts and stories about Nevada's history and people not found in most history books.

Victoria Sherrow, *Indians of the Plateau and Great Basin*. New York: Facts On File, 1992. Examines the life, history, and culture of early Native Americans in Nevada and surrounding states. Includes lots of photos and information on shelters, foods, tools, and clothing of these early inhabitants of Nevada and the Great Basin.

Bob Young, *Forged in Silver: The Story of the Comstock Lode*. New York: Messner, 1968. A readable version of the history of the Comstock Lode, including its discovery, its role in the Civil War, the people it made famous, and the suffering and tragedy it caused.

Websites

State of Nevada Department of Cultural Affairs (http://dmla.clan.lib.nv.us). This website has a special feature called "Nevada Kids Page," which has games, history, photos, more links, and a long list of books on Nevada for young readers.

The Public Broadcasting System (www.pbs.org). This site has links to a PBS series, *The American Experience*, which includes a show on the Donner Party. Details from survivors' diaries, photos, and commentary on the tragedy are included.

Index

Picture Credits

About the Author

Bob Anderson was a longtime editor for Greenhaven Press and Lucent Books. He is now a freelance writer and editor and Internet entrepreneur living in San Diego, California. He enjoys traveling in the United States and Mexico and going to Padres games.